Zoning Out

*Because zoning out
can get you dialed in*

By Thomas Guhr

Introduction

If I could harness the best smell in the world, it would be that of a freshly brewed cup of coffee. The steam rising up from the cup, encircling my nose and giving it a big kiss, like a smell character does in the cartoons. Now, to then drink that cup of coffee? No way! Rather, pour a glass of ice cold Dr. Pepper? Now we're talking. The burn of the carbonation in my throat, the sweetness on my tongue...greatness.

Greatness. Isn't that what we all want? To achieve the desires of our heart? What if I craved growth in my life like I craved the carbonation burn of Dr. Pepper? For me, Dr. Pepper represented comfort. Dr. Pepper was safe; Dr. Pepper was good. I knew what to expect. I knew where I could find it. I could have as much or as little as I wanted. I was in control. There was a time of my life where I didn't dare venture beyond the things that I knew. What lies outside the realm of Tom's simple mind? I don't know, that's why I didn't go there. Things were good . . . but how long is good, good enough?

A young woman has just graduated from nursing school and landed her first job on the cardiac unit. Being less than a year into her nursing career, she has been asked to take over as "Interim Head Nurse". She was told this role would be for six months while the manager was out on maternity leave. At the time, she was surprised by the request, but also pleased that her superiors and the medical director believed she was capable. It was a wonderful growth experience and, in it, she discovered that she loved being a leader while still being able to be involved with direct patient care; a calling she always felt on her life. Natalie would ultimately fulfill the role full-time and over the years that followed, the satisfaction she found in leading and managing a department, overseeing staff and nursing students, interacting with the whole team *and* caring for patients was incredibly rewarding. She would go on to be in this role for eleven years, some of the most rewarding and fulfilling years of her life.

In the pages to come, you'll find a series of stories, life experiences, that will take you on a journey of change and growth. These stories are likely no different than yours. We all have stories, but I hope the ones in this book will inspire you to think about what might come out of a life experience you've had, and that you'll absorb that outcome and apply it to the days ahead in your life in a meaningful way. Each of us are capable of achieving something great, but how do you unlock that greatness? Together we can create a revelation within you so that you can experience the amazing opportunities that life has to offer.

Whitesnake front man David Coverdale wrote these lyrics in his hit 80's rock song "Here I Go Again." "I don't know where I'm going, but I sure know where I've been," a clear description of what we're talking about in this book. The future is uncertain, but we see the past clearly. I compare this to driving a car. We have a rear-view mirror for a reason, to see clearly what's behind us. Challenging your comfort zone is like driving on a road you've never traveled; we need to press forward into the unknown with focus and not be fixated on what's behind us. We can't always play it safe just because it's familiar.

The stories ahead are a compilation of experiences, my personal experiences and experiences from others. These experiences did two things. First, they took me on a journey that taught me it's okay to be uncomfortable. Some of them flat-out shoved me off the edge of familiarity. Second, they taught me what stepping outside of a comfort zone looks like through someone else's eyes. A few of these stories along the way don't carry much profound weight, but they're good stories, and who doesn't love a good story.

I don't know about you, but when I think about challenging my comfort zone, I get kind of nervous. My stomach turns a little because, well, it makes me uncomfortable. There are two things I know about comfort zones. One, the walls of your zone are flexible. If you challenge them, they move and the more you push, the bigger they get. Two, your comfort zone can be moved and expanded by

others. The sequence must take place in that order. The walls of your comfort zone are yours, no one else's. They won't move if you're not ready for them to move.

Someone of influence can press you all day long, but only until you realize the significance of what they're asking and why it is they're asking it of you will your zone begin to widen. When was the last time you challenged your zone or allowed someone's influence to expand your zone because you knew what they were asking would move you toward unlocking a certain level of greatness in your life?

My hope is that you'll decide it's okay to press on the walls of your zone once in a while. Who knows, you might find an area of your life you didn't know existed. You might start zoning out.

The Hermit Crab

Did you ever know someone who had a hermit crab? Those little guys are fascinating creatures; creating a home inside of a shell only to vacate that space in search of a new larger one. Not only are they experts at knowing when it's time to grow; they're pros at navigating the vulnerable situations between shells. Like the hermit crab, if you choose to stay complacent, you'll end up resenting the self-imposed boundaries you've allowed to grow up around you. However, by allowing yourself freedom to grow, you too can learn to embrace discomfort.

Early Stretching

Let me start by telling you about meeting someone I would grow to love more than anything. More than basketball, video games and junk food; because let's be realistic, that's pretty much all there was to life as a teenager. I would become consumed by this person. Making this person happy would become one of my life purposes and the walls of my comfort zone would become forever expanded. Before I tell you about this person, however, I need to rewind and set the stage of my life for you.

I recently retold a certain time in my life during a conversation with a new-found connection in my professional sphere. We were discussing spiritual matters when he asked me to describe what life was like for me before I came to know Jesus. I was five years old, sitting in the Sunday School room of a small country church. The church sat at the end of a pine tree lined drive, in the beautiful Ozark mountains of Arkansas. This church was simple, yet majestic, set in a picturesque and sometimes fog-filled valley. The type of setting you'd see on a postcard as you walk through a visitor's center somewhere or see by the register on the counter of a gas station. For my family, it was a place we visited regularly. It was a Sunday evening, we had already been there that morning and the Wednesday evening before that and then the Sunday before that, you're catching on. We were in church a lot. Church was part of my parents' identity; therefore, it was also part of mine. On that Sunday evening, in a room smaller than the size of a standard bedroom, Jesus took hold of my life. I explained to my new friend that I haven't known a life without Christ. Christ has always been with me, guiding me, building me and preparing me for the road ahead.

After concluding our time together, I reflected on our conversation. As I drove, it occurred to me, Christ was the first game-changer in my life, although I had no notion of that when I was five years old in that old country church. My comfort zone was set on a track that would stretch far beyond what I thought would be possible.

Chapter 1

This Pull was Tough

It was sophomore year, 1998. My family and I lived in rural America, Elbing, Kansas. "Small town" doesn't even describe its size. As of the 2010 census, Elbing's population was 229. I lived there for only a few years, but those years had a powerful effect on me. Elbing sat smack in the middle of Kansas farmland, and was known primarily for a grain elevator and a school called Berean Academy.

During harvest season, Elbing would crawl with farm trucks. Farmers from all over the area would bring their trucks full of harvested grain direct from the field to

Elbing, where it would be stored in one of eight to ten

grain elevators. Farming in Kansas was a major part of the

economy, and bringing your crop in for storage played a

key role in the outcome of your livelihood. When a farmer

arrives at the elevator, his truck is weighed on a giant

scale, and a sampling of the crop is processed. One major

part of processing is checking for moisture. In order to

store grain, the moisture content needs to be around 15%.

If moisture is higher, the grain might mold. If it's lower, the

grain might be too dry. If the grain is too wet, then the

farmer has to pay to have it dried, therefore lowering the

cost paid per bushel. From there, the grain is dumped from

the truck down into an underground bin where it is taken

to the silo by a continuously running conveyor belt. Once

the grain reaches the bin, it is taken to the top of the silo by buckets, therefore inheriting the name grain elevator.

After the truck is empty, it is then weighed again to

determine how much crop has been deposited to the

elevator. The process goes on from here, but I'll stop.

When I lived in Elbing, those grain elevators didn't mean

much, just an area of town that carried the continuous

hum of belt motors and dump truck engines creating a

seemingly ever-present dust cloud driven by a steady

Kansas wind. I look back now and realize how important a

role that process played for many people. Their livelihood

depended upon Elbing.

Berean Academy sat directly at the south end of

town. It was known for its outstanding academics and rich

sporting history. My parents and both uncles went to

school there, and in the sixth grade, I became a student

there as well. When it came to sports, my family was right

in the middle. For a long time, my uncle Mike held, and still may hold, the record for most points scored in a basketball game, 50 . . . before there was a three-point line. My other uncle, Les, shattered a glass backboard on a dunk during practice. Breakaway rims weren't a thing yet. And my dad? He was a last-second hero during a key game at the end of the season. Down by one, his teammate heaved up a long shot to win the game but came up short. My dad caught the ball and scored as time expired! I ran track, primarily the 400-meter run and triple jump. I also played soccer and basketball. Basketball was always my go-to sport because of my height. Having grown seven inches during the summer between my sixth and seventh grade years gave me a big advantage in the paint.

As a sixth grader, our class participated in the "hundred-mile" club. Each day at recess, we had the option to run on the track, or do something else. Those students who traversed one hundred miles by the end of the school year would be privy to a movie and soda on the last day before summer break, a pretty good incentive. Having an opportunity to skip out on a half day's school work was a no-brainer. I was determined for my last day not to consist of anything that remotely resembled school, so I completed the hundred miles, one lap around the track at a time. Kind of a neat foreshadowing to accomplishing something great in your life huh? Along with the accomplishment of running a hundred miles over the span of eight and a half months came the development of Osgood-Schlatter's, a painful lump that forms just below the kneecap. I remember going home at the end of the day and icing my knees. Osgood-Schlatter's is the result of repetitive motion during childhood. It doesn't bother me much these days, but back then it sure did.

Elbing holds many memories for me, probably because those were my developing years. My friends and I were rarely inside. We were always together and always getting into something. One summer, we invented, I'll say we invented it, the game of "dunk ball." It was awesome! Basically, you lower the basketball goal down to eight feet and play with a ball the size of a cantaloupe. It was every man (boy) for themselves and goal tending was allowed, so pretty much the only way to score was to drive in and dunk. It was fierce! Sometimes my best friend and I would play one-on-one basketball until three in the morning, first one to a hundred. Other times we were running football passing routes at 11 p.m. by street light. I recall one time, some friends and I were down at the ponds. The ponds were an area just outside of town where waste water was kept. We used to shoot skeet (clay pigeons) there, play in the hedge rows, walk the train tracks, ride bikes, etc. This particular time, though, we were with an older friend, a friend who could drive. When we decided to leave, I was in the back seat, and he decided that would be a good day to drive out of the pond area in reverse. The dirt road down to the ponds from the main blacktop was long and straight, a football field in length. I'm not sure how fast you can go in reverse, but it felt like we were flying! When we got to the road, he tried to do one of those spinning drift moves you see in the movies where the nose of the car swings around with the tires screeching, the driver slamming the car into drive and speeding forward without missing a beat. But when he went to hit the brakes, there weren't any, and we ended up backward in the bottom of a 14-foot drainage ditch. When the chaos of the moment ended and

the car wasn't upside down, I remember thinking I could've

reached out the back window and touched the ground. The

only thing that kept the car from rolling over onto its top

was the undercarriage getting hung up on a culvert. The

car stayed there for months, his dad refusing to pull it out.

Someone even put a "no parking" sign out by the road. It

was funny later, not at the time.

Another memory of Elbing was playing golf with

tennis balls. We'd start at one end of town and say, "okay,

you know that tree at the other end of town? First one to

hit it in the least number of strokes wins." We went

through people's yards, front or back. Or down the middle

of the street.

One day I was home alone, I don't remember why,

but I can still vividly recall going outside to see the sky a shade of dark green in the middle of the afternoon.

Remember, we were in central Kansas. The clouds were

doing this weird spiral movement and it was oddly calm.

We lived in a mobile home so there wasn't much shelter to

take. I would've texted my parents, but you know, that

tech didn't exist yet. I got on my bike and rode across town

to a friend's house who had a basement, only to get there

and find they weren't home either. By that time, I was

beginning to get worried as I rode back across town. The

clouds didn't turn into a tornado that day, just some rain,

but it still shook me.

In the picture above, you'll see the grain elevators

on the right, the east side of town. Grain elevators were

typically located in small towns, providing closer proximity for the farmer. They were usually placed along a rail or water way. You can see the train tracks that run along the east side of town. At the bottom of the picture, you'll see Berean Academy. I ran 400 laps around that track. In the picture, there are three main streets that run parallel to each other. My house was along the rightmost street (main street) in the upper third, northern portion of town. At the very top right corner, a white road disappears out of the frame. That's where my daring friend decided a reverse exit would be a good idea.

During those years, life in Elbing was all I needed. We went to the bigger towns for food, for church, and to see family, but other than that, we didn't need to leave.

I don't recall the exact evening but I remember my parents sitting my sister and I down to tell us we were moving. Um . . . what? Not to the next town, or out into the country. No, we were moving out of the state! I'm pretty sure my best friend was like, "Dude, you should just live with me and then when we graduate in a couple years you can go live with your parents." I remember checking the box on the form they give you on the last day of school; **will you be returning next year?** *Please circle yes or no.* Circling no was a scary thought. I was in my middle teen years, all my friends were here, I ran track and played on the junior varsity basketball team. (We went undefeated that year by the way.) I played in the band, and probably had a crush on a girl in my class. The thought of moving was outside the chances of a possibility, but my

23

parents respected our space and gave us some time to let that thought sink in. I was comfortable . . .

Jeremiah 29:11 - "For I know the plans I have for you, declares the Lord. Plans to prosper you and not to harm you, plans to give you hope and a future." – NIV

Proverbs 16:9 – "In their hearts humans plan their course, but the Lord establishes their steps." – NIV

God had a plan for my life long before I was born and He was about to guide the steps for the next part of our journey.

As I sat on my bed that night, did I make a conscious decision to be open to change? "I, Tom, am the kind of person who is open to change!" No, that didn't happen. My comfort zone was on the verge of change and I didn't know it. When my parents told me and my sister about the move, I immediately turned off to the idea. I did

not volunteer for this. (A recurring theme, you'll see.)

However, that feeling didn't last too long. I told my friends

we were moving, and we left. I was okay, life went on, and

my comfort zone expanded.

TIP: Be open to the idea of challenging your comfort zone.

A willing and open mind is a powerful tool. Remember, the

walls of your comfort zone are flexible. Simply having an

open mind will put you in a ready state for change and

even if you are involuntarily pulled from your comfort

zone, you may think differently about your current

situation.

In 1992, a young police detective was called into

Bill's office, Bill was the Deputy Chief of Police, Clayton was the young detective. Clayton lived in a small town in Northern Oklahoma with a population just over 25,000. Bill told him he had been assigned to give a series of speeches to a group in town. Giving speeches was not in Clayton's sphere of comfort. He hesitated, immediately feeling uneasy at the thought. Clayton thrived on working alone and sometimes with a small team he knew really well. Standing in front of strangers had absolutely no appeal to him. As he told me this story, Clayton said that in college he'd rather have taken 13 credit hours of something else than a three-hour course on public speaking. Sounds a lot like many people I know, myself included. There's a duel going on here. Clayton's unease with public speaking matched with the Deputy Chief requesting a task of his subordinate. Neither of them refusing to give. What would you do in this situation? You've just been asked by a superior to do something that ramps up your anxiety levels, not morally or ethically, you just don't want to do it out of fear of the unknown. Clayton was facing a dilemma that he knew he'd need to overcome. He soon realized there was no escaping this work assignment, so he accepted and began to prepare. He had a couple of weeks to get ready, and he took full advantage. If he was going to stand up in front of strangers, you better believe he was going to know his material. The inevitable day came and he started his first of four speeches. "That first one was a little rocky out of sheer fear, but fear soon surrendered to confidence," Clayton recalled. By the time he was giving the third and fourth talks, he was starting to enjoy himself. He was confident in the material, he was confident in himself, and he began to get audience members involved. The classic movie How the Grinch Stole Christmas, contains this famous line from the narrator: "They say that the Grinch's small heart grew three sizes that day." Well, Clayton's comfort zone did the same thing. He was involuntarily pushed out of his comfort zone. The walls of his zone, like yours, are flexible. Someone else pressed on them for him, which is incredibly uncomfortable. Had his boss allowed him to duck that assignment, he likely never would have overcome his fear of public speaking. That fear would have hindered his career and he would have plateaued professionally. Since then, he has obtained two positions at the highest level in his profession, Chief of Police and United States Marshal. Neither would have happened if he had yielded to his fear of public speaking.

On September 24, 1789, the Judiciary Act was approved by Congress and signed into law by President George Washington. Washington then appointed the first

13 U.S. Marshals. Today, there are 94 Marshals in the United States, one for each federal judicial district.

Marshals continue to be appointed by the President of the United States and in 2008, Clayton was appointed by President Barak Obama, becoming a part of this storied branch in law enforcement.

Have you had a "Bill" push you out of your comfort zone? For me, that Bill was my parents in 1998. It's okay to wince at the thought of being asked to do something uncomfortable. Process the request and look for areas of growth and opportunity. If there is an upside to their request, then I challenge you to resist the urge to "duck the assignment."

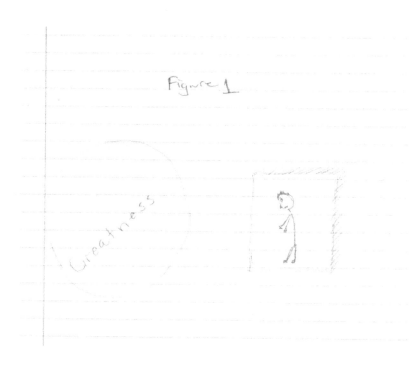

Figure 1

This figure shows a place in life we are all familiar with. The

character inside his or her comfort zone frustrated at the

current state of their life. They can see greatness ahead

but for some reason, they feel stuck. However, the

character is standing, not giving up and ready to continue forward.

"Great things never came from comfort zones."

-Ben Francia

You may or may not have heard the quote above. It was the first quote I read that really got me thinking on this subject. At the time, I was coaching individuals who were trying to make a positive life change. Many aspects of the work we were doing together were difficult, but that work was paying off with BIG TIME rewards, rewards that some of these people had sought after their entire lives. As I was preparing for a coaching session one evening, I came across that quote and immediately formed that week's session around it. Just as I was coaching life change for those people, the people in the stories you've read had the

drive and desire to grow. The walls of their comfort zones

are flexible, just like yours.

Chapter 2

The Move Back

Let's face a reality together, if we may. When you leave your comfort zone, it'll be hard, you'll feel uneasy and your feathers might get ruffled. Here's what I've learned from that so far. It's okay. Once you move a portion of your zone, that area now becomes your new normal.

When I was a kid, between the ages of three and nine, we lived in Arkansas because my parents ran a camp. Not just any camp, Ponca Bible Camp. This camp was amazing and it played a key role, not only in my life, but in the lives of many kids throughout the years. This camp was a summertime staple to kids of my generation, my parents' generation, and a generation before them. Each July, hundreds of kids would pour in and out of this camp. Friendships were rekindled from the summer before and new friendships were formed. Camp meant connection; connection with each other, to nature and to Jesus.

We spent time each day playing, eating, swimming, studying the Bible and just being together. We even cleaned up after each other. Each cabin group would rotate time cleaning the kitchen and dining hall after each meal. Some cabins picked up trash on the grounds, some swept out the outdoor chapel and some cleaned the shower house. At the end of each meal, the camp director would announce the KP (kitchen patrol) duties and assign a cabin. There was always one cabin with no cleaning assignment. All the kids crossed their fingers, hoping they'd be part of that cabin, and it rotated so there was always a chance that if you cleaned something the meal before, you might get out of it the next meal. This time not only taught us responsibility, but it taught us to have each other's backs and look out for one another. Let's be honest here, I didn't get that message at the time, nor did probably anyone else. All we wanted to do was play and swim.

Swimming was a daily occurrence at camp. In mid-afternoon, we would hike down to the swimming hole. This swimming spot was part of the Buffalo River, a public access point in the Buffalo National Park. At this particular juncture in the river, the water pooled because of a small bridge making it the perfect swimming spot. I spent a lot of time there as a kid (I lived there remember), and during these summer weeks, I got to share it with all my friends during camp.

Another staple during camp was going caving. Arkansas has many great opportunities to explore caves. One cave in particular, we dubbed the bat cave, had a place that not many people went. It was called the "birth canal," no need to expand here, but you'll understand why it got its name. Every year, a certain brave group of kids would venture on a guided tour to this section of the cave. This one particular summer, I was ready to take on the challenge. To enter, you had to shimmy through a hole in the side of the cave wall the size of roughly two to three basketballs. Once inside, you made your way down a four-foot drop onto a small landing that would hold no more than two people, then down another three to four foot drop into a small room the size of the half bath in your home. In the corner of this room, was the entrance to the birth canal, a chute that seemed a mile long. Realistically it was probably 40-50 feet long. We entered this chute single file laying on our stomachs. Put yourself here for a second. It's pitch dark, cold and wet. Now, you lay on your belly and begin to inch yourself forward with your toes. In front of you are a pair of shoes, behind you is someone's head. You're pushing forward through rocks, puddles of water and mud. There are places in this chute, no joke, where your shoes, or your head for that matter, cannot be straight up and down. In that moment, you cannot let yourself get out of your head. You keep moving forward and pray the person in front you do the same. After getting through the birth canal, you're opened up into a great room! This room was filled with stalactites and stalagmites. There were places on the cave wall where water had run for many years creating different textures. It was amazing! Something that I never would have seen anywhere else. To exit this amazing place was the same experience as entering. You guessed it, back through the birth canal, but this time it didn't seem so long, and while you relied on yourself to get down, there were now people to pull you up and out. Our clothes were pretty much ruined and unrecognizable, so to clean off, we stopped at the swimming hole, just mentioned above, and jumped in fully clothed. Still, those clothes were done. I had gone to this camp for years; in fact, unlike others who traveled in from out of state on a bus, I actually lived there. I had these experiences at my fingertips each and every day, yet I was still scared of the unknown.

This happens to us all of the time. When was the last time you stepped out and did something different or challenging that was right in your backyard, so to speak; and once you did, you found that it opened up a whole new world you didn't know existed? To set the record straight, that was first and only time I would venture through the bat cave birth canal. Once was enough and even though it was a one-and-done type of experience for me, it taught me that new opportunities are all around us. We just need to challenge ourselves to step out.

TIP: Another way to challenge your comfort zone is to challenge yourself. The walls of your zone are flexible but you won't know how flexible unless you know how strong you can push.

"As you get older, you look back and you understand how you became the person you are."

– Michael Jordan

Chapter 3

Inconvenience

So you might be thinking about where the walls of your zone lie. Awesome! I commend you for that. Let me also mention that when you test them, you may experience inconveniences along the way.

When I was in my early thirties, I had the opportunity to travel out of state. At the time, I was in the healthcare/wellness industry, and I was headed to the sunshine state for a three-day conference. The trip to the conference went rather smoothly. We departed from

Tulsa, Oklahoma, connected in Atlanta and then it was on to Orlando. The remainder of the trip was great, until I experienced a few setbacks on the way home. Many of you reading have your own airport stories or know someone who does. Well, this is my airport story.

My return flight was scheduled to leave Orlando at 6:30 p.m. on a Friday evening. I scheduled my ride from the hotel to the airport to pick me up at 2 p.m. It was a 30-minute drive to the airport which would put me there at around 2:30 p.m. leaving plenty of time to for me to make it through the TSA checks and to my gate. Well, things were moving smoothly; I made it to my gate with plenty of time to spare, I even had time to grab some dinner and strike up a conversation with a fellow traveler. Then about thirty minutes before our plane was set to arrive at the gate there was an announcement overhead. "Ladies and gentlemen, there has been a slight disturbance at the main corridor of the airport, we thank you for your patience."

Ok, no cause for alarm, just keep hanging out. About five minutes later, again the flight attendant came on with an update. "Ladies and gentlemen, the slight disturbance has increased in severity, we will keep you up to date as we receive more information." Hmmm...starting to wonder a little. Those sitting around me start looking at each other. Meanwhile, the plane we were set to board had landed and was approaching the gate. It was approximately 6pm at this point and a few minutes later came another update. "Your attention please, the plane approaching the gate will be halted and the unloading of this aircraft will not take place at this moment until the issue in the main airport corridor has been resolved, again we thank you for your patience." Ok, now we're starting to get a tad restless, people are wiggling in their chairs, they're pulling their belongings close, and some are starting to move about. A few minutes later, at approximately 6:45 p.m., we get another update. "The disturbance at TSA check and pre-check has been upgraded to severe. We will unload the approaching plane but will not be boarding at this time." Yeah, you guessed it, more talking and pacing. As the plane I was supposed to be boarding is unloading, we get another update. "Ladies and gentleman, all passengers please make your way back to the main hub of the airport. All passengers will have to go back through TSA check. Please gather your belongings and move that direction in an orderly fashion." Orderly? Not so much. I felt like I was on the verge of being in a stampede.

Side note, I don't know if you've ever been in the Orlando airport, but it's not the easiest airport to navigate.

Let me paint a picture for you if I could. Picture a centralized location, your house for example, your house is where people enter from the outside to check in, get their tickets, check their bags, peruse gift shops, go to the restroom, eat, etc. It's also where people arriving on planes go to exit the airport. Ok, from your house there are two arms. One arm goes out at 45-degree angle to the right and the other to the left. These arms are quite lengthy with options to both ride a train or walk and take you to your desired gate. There are many gates for plane entry and departure at the ends of these arms. Now, imagine the amount of people at the end of each arm coming back to the house and joining people who are currently in the house trying to get out to the arms. Chaos is a good way to put it.

Once I made it back to the concourse, I proceeded to stand for more than two hours with a couple thousand people. Some people sitting, most standing. People charging their phones and other devices. Remember, a lot of people don't print flight tickets anymore, they are stored on their phones, and every charging port was taken.

So, what happened to cause all of this? Well, while I was sitting at the gate waiting for my plane, someone's bag going through the TSA check began to smoke. That bag then popped and people scattered. Some people ran backward into the concourse, some people ran through the metal detectors; anywhere they could go because they just heard something explode. Because of this, security couldn't be sure if it was an accident or a distraction of some kind, so everyone who was beyond the TSA checkpoint had to return and go back through. The "pop" in the bag was a lithium battery. So, as we waited in the concourse, security, local police and fire departments scoured every inch of the arms and gate area of the airport for anything suspicious (hence the two hours of standing). At times I was squatting, at other times standing on one leg, doing whatever I could to keep myself from turning into a stiff board. All the while people continued to funnel into the airport, unaware of the dilemma we faced on the inside.

Finally, we were moving again. It was somewhat orderly as we went back through the TSA checkpoints, but once we got beyond that, people began to run, trying to get back to their plane and on to their destination. I made it back to where I started and boarded at around midnight. We departed Orlando and arrived in Atlanta an hour or so later, only to find (what shouldn't have come to my surprise) that my connecting flight to Tulsa had left a long time ago. Guess I'd be spending the night in the airport. That was a long night, but it's interesting to see an airport without the hustle and bustle of travel. I spent most of the night at the gate in which I thought I was supposed to be, the one that would take me to Tulsa the next morning. At around 5 a.m. Saturday morning, I realized that the gate I was at was no longer the right gate, so I had to find my way to the correct place. I approached the woman at the desk, explained my ordeal from the night before, and basically wanted to ensure that my previously purchased ticket was still valid for my return flight. Not only was it still correct, but she bumped me up to first class! Yes! I'd never flown first class before. A couple hours later the "all call" was made and we began to board. I made it to my seat, holy cow the leg room! I'm six feet four inches tall, leg room on a flight is a must, big smile! I was getting comfortable in my seat (come on Tom, not too comfortable) and settling in for my flight home. The plane was three quarters of the way full when a voice came overhead. "Ladies and gentlemen, this is your captain speaking. We are having a minor electrical delay in the cockpit, just sit tight and I'll keep you updated." Ok, I thought, I've been through this before very recently, everything's fine. A few minutes later, "Ladies and gentlemen, this is your captain again, due to the electrical malfunctions we are experiencing in the cockpit, we are going to ask you to gather your belongings, leave the plane and return to your seats in the airport gate. We will be getting another plane for you soon and you'll be on your way to Tulsa." OH COME ON!! That was my internal thought, but we exited and waited for a different plane. An hour and a half later, another plane arrived and I boarded in my original order of coach seating. My chance at first class now null and void. Not only was I ready to be home, but my son was turning six this day, and I couldn't miss that. After many hours behind schedule, I made it home in time to see him have a great birthday, and quite a story to tell my family.

The contrast of this story has the same outcome with a completely different journey along the way. I tell the story in this manner, so you'll see just how important a role mindset plays when the walls of your comfort zones are moved with a force outside of your control, such as the delays I experienced on this trip.

The discomfort starts at the boarding gate with the announcement that there's been a slight disturbance in the main hub of the airport. "Are you kidding me?" I could've thought, "You can never have a smooth flying experience start to finish." My attitude turning negative, and I slump down in my chair. With each announcement that follows, my attitude becoming more and more negative and I start complaining to the person in the seat next to me, pointing a finger at the flight attendant as if they are directly to blame for this delay. When I hear the announcement that we'll all have to clear the boarding gate area and go back to the main terminal, the volume of my complaining elevates and now spreads to anyone who will listen. As we make our way back to the main hub, my pace is quick and my movements harsh, dashing and bumping into people. When I make it back to where we were instructed to go, I find that all of my haste was in vain because now I have to stand and wait for security to give the all-clear. Now I'm really mad! I'm tired because I just tried to beat everyone back to the front. My legs hurt and there's nowhere to sit. I can't even sit on the ground because there are so many people. All I can do is stand. Oh, and my phone battery is going dead because it hasn't been on a charger since the night before and my plane ticket is on my phone. With each passing minute, I become more restless and on the constant lookout for a vacant port to charge my phone. By this time, the people around me are ignoring me and giving me dirty looks because they are in the same boat as I am, and they don't want to hear me venting about how terrible this is. Finally, we start moving. "It's about time," I say out loud. We arrive in the Atlanta airport only to find that my plane to Tulsa has already left. Great, looks like I'll have to sleep in the airport. I rustle around and try to get comfortable. I try to sleep sitting up, but of course I can't because the cleaning crew keeps driving by with their floor shining equipment. As morning arrives, I lean over to the person next to me and continue my complaint-filled rant about the night before. Well, to my amazement after a frustrated discussion with the flight attendant, I get bumped up to first-class for enduring my prior troubles. "Things are slowly starting to turn," I think to myself. After finding my seat in first-class, I'm now told the plane has some type of electrical malfunction. We are told to get off and wait for another plane. I start complaining again to my fellow first-class passengers and proceed to make sure they know about the previous 16 hours I've had and how terrible it's been. They don't want to hear about it which perturbs me even more. When we are allowed to board the "new" plane, I find that I have been moved back to coach, as my original ticket showed. You better believe the flight attendant got an ear full for that. We finally land in Tulsa and when I see my family, all I can do is rant and rave about how terrible my entire trip was with the birthday party being an after thought.

"Once your mindset changes, everything on the outside will change along with it."

-Steve Maraboli

TIP: Just because the walls of your comfort zone are flexible doesn't mean they're easily moved. You need to be aware that there will be obstacles along the way, but more importantly, your mindset will determine whether your comfort zone expands or not. Scott Alexander put this into an interesting light when he said in his book Rhinoceros Success that the key to success is naturally to become a rhinoceros. A rhinoceros you say? That's right, because a rhinoceros knows what it wants. A rhino is extremely focused. Once a rhino has a purpose, it charges with all its might, and while it's charging, there's nothing that stands in its way because a rhinoceros has two-inch thick skin. You get his point, simply know that there will be obstacles on your path to achieving your goals, but guess what? You have two-inch thick skin and the walls of your comfort zone are flexible; you either absorb those obstacles as learning opportunities, or they just bounce right off and you keep going!

Chapter 4

Purpose-filled Expansion

Contentment

This book is about challenging the flexible walls of your comfort zone. Yes, it's important for us to be in a continual state of mind where we're looking to grow and learn, but don't translate that into meaning that if you're not pushing, then you're not growing. It's ok to be content. Contentment is such a valuable asset in today's culture, and I hope to portray that contentment and a challenged comfort zone are in the same family. Webster's dictionary defines contentment as a state of happiness and satisfaction, and I would also add to that, saying that you're in a state of enjoyment of your current situation. There is something deep down inside of me that always wants to push and grow continually. However, I've found that when I slow down and enjoy the fruits of that "go go go" mentality, true bliss is found. Think of your own situation. Where are you? Are you in a state of contentment all of the time, rarely challenging yourself? Are you super comfortable? Or do you find you're at the other end of the spectrum, in a constant state of "go go go," rarely spending time to stop and enjoy what you've accomplished? I encourage you to find that middle ground where the two mentalities are married together on a consistent basis.

Forced Expansion

I have found, and likely so have you, that when I get into zone expansion mode, it's hard to scale back. This is where I experience discontent. I become fixated on the "what if?" If I just push harder, I'll be more successful, I'll make more money, I'll get done faster, I'll be more satisfied, I'll be happier. How often do we get caught in this trap? I caution you not to push for expansion when it doesn't feel right. Two examples that drive this point home.

Example ONE

I read a quote, probably a meme on social media, that said, "you can't expect a hole by leaning against the shovel." I took this to mean that we do need to put in the work, we do need to be motivated, but don't continually dig in one place to create one massive hole. Instead, find a state in which you are satisfied, admire your work and then dig another hole. In other words, find purpose when you're pushing to expand your comfort zone. Expanding your zone for the sake of simply having a bigger zone will not bring you as much fulfillment as if you were to make smaller strategic pushes that are fueled with purpose. This is where true contentment will be found as you continue to grow.

Example TWO

As the high school students entered the school, the principal handed them a balloon. The principal instructed them to write their name on the balloon and place it in a certain hallway in the school. After third hour, the principal announced over the intercom system for each student to go to that particular hallway. Once everyone had arrived, the students were given five minutes to find their balloon. Kids were moving all over the place, balloons were flying everywhere, being kicked, hit and grabbed from one another; it was chaos. At the end of the five minutes, with the exception of maybe a couple, the vast majority of students could not find their balloon. The principal then instructed the students to pick up the balloon next to them. They were then given five minutes to find that person and give them their balloon. At the end of the five minutes, each student had his own balloon back. The principal explained that the balloon represents happiness, that if you go out in search of your own happiness, it will be incredibly difficult to find. However, if you go out in life searching to bring someone else happiness, you will find your happiness in return.

The same can be said for comfort zone expansion. Yes, you can expand your own comfort zone. But remember, the walls of your zone are flexible, and along the way, turn your focus to others and how you can help them expand their zone. Who knows, maybe you'll find increased purpose and fulfillment in your own comfort zone expansion journey.

Chapter 5

New Life

Part 1

I knew it was important to continue my education

after graduating from high school, so I enrolled at the local

community college. Basketball continued to be a main

focus for me, and I made the basketball team as a walk-on.

I had a great first year, practicing and traveling with the

team. That next summer, I got a good job working for the

U.S. Postal Service, so making money soon became more appealing than playing basketball. My job with the Postal Service was a temporary one-year job, I knew that going in, so after a year it was on to the next thing. That next thing was a factory job working nights, eleven at night to seven in the morning. I'd get off work at seven, go to my apartment, shower, attend college classes until noon and sleep from one in the afternoon until around seven that evening. I'd then eat dinner and go back to work. Put that cycle on repeat and throw in spending as much time as I could with my girlfriend, and that was my life.

TIME OUT!

In the first paragraph of Early Stretching, before chapter one, I referenced a person who I would grow to love more than anything; enter Rose Ellis. She was new to the community college, and we met through a mutual friend. One day, we were all sitting around a table in the student union, talking between classes and sliding each other's cell phones back and forth. I know . . . exciting stuff. Her phone landed in front of me, so I opened it up and put my phone number in it. Smooth, right? A few weeks later, she and a friend were shopping and ended up getting locked out of their car. As she looked through her phone to decide who to call, what number did she come across? Mine. That moment kick-started a slow transition that would turn into us spending more and more time together. Once while we were dating, I was at work on my birthday (night shift to jog your memory). It was just about time for "lunch," if lunch can be at three o'clock on the morning. Someone told me that something was wrong with my car. I went out to check on it and it was covered in toilet paper, shaving cream and streamers. Her car was next to mine, and she was inside her car with a warm pizza. A moment I'll never forget. Our relationship has been full of moments, many shared in this book. One moment in particular took place one hundred feet in the air. One of our first dates began with the hunt for a haunted house. We drove with some friends for a couple hours without success. On the way home we decided to stop and climb a lookout tower. It was a cool November night, the air was clear and crisp, you could see for miles. I managed to work up the courage to put my arm around her. I didn't know how she was going to respond, but I had to go for it. It went well. One year to the day that we climbed the lookout tower on that cold November night, we returned to the top of that tower. Instead of putting my arm around her, I got on one knee. From that day forward, my comfort zone became her comfort zone.

TIP: Challenging your comfort zone will open up new opportunities. Sometimes those new opportunities will have an impact on others. The flexible walls of your comfort zone can collide with the flexible walls of others. Also, be keenly aware that it's important to surround yourself with people who will push you when you're getting too comfortable.

Part 2

After we got married, we moved to Russellville, Arkansas to continue advancing toward our undergraduate degrees. Rose majored in Early Childhood Education, and I took courses in Wellness and Fitness Management. Shortly after beginning our new lives in a new place, three plus hours from our nearest family members, we found out Rose was pregnant. Our comfort zones just got rocked, as we were now set to be new parents and attending school full-time. Rose's pregnancy was less than optimal, like far less. The first twenty weeks of morning sickness rivaled any illness I had seen, it's difficult to put into words. As her husband, new husband at that, it killed me to see my new bride in that shape, but let me tell you, my wife is a ROCKSTAR. She switched her college plan to part-time and eventually her health turned toward the better; time passed and we were in the hospital ready to meet the newest member of our family. After an extensive, exhaustive and painful 23-hour labor, our daughter Zita (pronounced Zee-tah) Dawn was born. When she made her entrance into this world, her first attempted breath was fluid, not oxygen causing a small hole to puncture her lung. She was diagnosed with a pneumothorax. We were in the hospital an additional week and a half, because Zita was in the NICU. Rose even had to receive several units of blood due to the loss of blood during the delivery. It was a scary time, but both made speedy recoveries, and we were able to head home. From there, Rose and I alternated class schedules. She would attend class on Tuesdays and Thursdays while I stayed home. She would then stay home on Monday, Wednesday and Friday so I could attend classes.

One night when Zita was just shy of her first birthday, she cut in her first front tooth and Rose had a big exam the next morning. Zita woke me up in the night, as babies tend to do, but this night she was not feeling well, so we went to the couch. She was crying uncontrollably so I put her on my knee and began bouncing her. That worked! She was calm and then fell asleep. Many parents with a newborn will know the next sequence of moves; you SLOWLY slide the baby toward you because I dare not wake her up. I got her about mid-thigh from my knee when she woke up screaming so back to the knee she went. This cycle continued for what seemed like, and probably was, hours. Knee to thigh to chest, knee to thigh to chest. After falling asleep on my knee, I got her to my chest, still asleep, then to her crib, STILL ASLEEP. Then I got to the door, then to my bed. But as fate would have it that night, she wouldn't sleep. Eventually, I gave up trying to get any sleep and we both camped out on the couch. That was a LONG night, and yet another initiation to fatherhood.

It's funny how we remember certain things in our lives. In the book Power of Moments, Chip and Dan Heath write about moments being peaks and pits. I'd definitely say that was a pit moment, but one we look back on and chuckle about. As I recall that time in our lives, I think to myself. *How did we do that?* Just kids ourselves in our early twenties. We raised a child in the midst of the busyness of attending school full-time and working jobs. We were definitely stretched, sometimes to the max, but we kept on moving forward.

After graduating, we moved a couple hours away to settle into the next phase of our lives, and bought our first home as a family. A few short years later we welcomed another member to our family, our second daughter Zoe. I find it interesting how certain life experiences shape your perceptions of a similar experience previously in your life. In this example, the entire process of having a baby. The pregnancy, the trip to the hospital, the labor, the delivery, the recovery time, the going home, etc. Rose's pregnancy with Zoe was very similar to that of Zita. Horrible morning sickness, but yet again, Rose is a ROCKSTAR. She got through it and the morning sickness subsided. Rose was very near the 40-week mark in her pregnancy, everything was going smoothly, she felt well and we had our hospital bag packed and by the front door. I had been invited to a baseball game nearby and we decided it would be okay for me to go. Well, as fate would have it, Rose called me during the seventh-inning-stretch to say she had started having contractions. Of course I went into full-on panic mode, telling her I was on my way. We had to go to the hospital right now! Rose, on the other hand, was more relaxed. "Finish the game, and when you get home, we'll see how far apart the contractions are," she said. I couldn't do that. I told my friend I had to go. When I got home, her contractions were close enough together that we decided to go to the hospital anyway. Rose's dad came and took Zita home with him and we settled in for what I was prepared for, a very very long and exhaustive labor experience. We had a restful night. Rose was comfortable (thank you epidural) and we had a fantastic nurse. She progressed smoothly through the night and into the next day. Then, at one o'clock in the afternoon, with three pushes, Zoe was here. I distinctly remember thinking to myself, "we're done?" I say that because with Zita, Rose's epidural didn't work and the anesthesiologist refused to come back in and fix it or put in a new one. With Zoe, the epidural worked perfectly. With Zita, Rose labored for 23 hours, the final two hours of that pushing. With Zoe, the epidural masked her contractions and she pushed three times. To put this into a sport analogy, because that's what

I do, we were hunkered down and ready for a marathon when we ended up with a 5k. Rose, I love you more than you'll ever know.

The takeaway for me here is that we ended up with two amazing daughters who have immensely blessed our lives, but they came in two completely different ways. I was shown that just because one experience plays out a certain way doesn't mean that every similar experience thereafter will follow the same pattern.

TIP: When you decide to challenge your comfort zone, two things are certain. First, you won't always know you're in the midst of a "comfort zone change." It's only with time that you'll look back and realize that the course of your life was stretching your flexible comfort zone walls for you. Second, you won't always experience immediate results, but keep moving forward. The walls of your comfort zone are flexible, sometimes producing easy wins and other times not producing hardly anything. When this happens, new life experiences are taking place and shaping you even if you don't feel it. In fact, what if you feel like you're often being pushed rather than the one doing the pushing. Like some force of life is moving you beyond your comfort level and you need a break! I've had the honor of getting to know individuals during the course of my life who've shared instances just like this with me. One of those individuals is Jill.

Jill was born with a genetic disease, a disease that has a life expectancy tied to it. Her entire life has been spent trying to beat it and to prove "them" wrong. She had some close calls throughout her younger years, but she always pulled through. When she was 22 years old, she received a bilateral lung transplant. There is also a life expectancy with lung transplants, so once again she was fighting to beat the odds. For the 20 years after her transplant, she did great. She had the lungs of a person born with normally functioning lungs. She ran half marathons, hiked in the mountains, traveled overseas, received a Master's degree, had a successful career and married the man of her dreams. Life was perfect. Then in 2018, things changed. She was diagnosed with lymphoma, cancer caused by the drugs used to suppress her immune system after the transplant. She could easily say that cancer pushed her out of her comfort zone, again, but she continued to handle this diagnosis as she did most things, with faith and fight, and it was her mentality that beat the cancer. Soon after she was announced to be cancer-free, she and her medical team were faced with yet another difficult decision, whether to resume immunosuppression and risk a reoccurrence of cancer, or not and risk rejection of her lungs. After much deliberation, it was decided to not put her back on the medication that caused the lymphoma. She did okay for a few months, but then began to experience the effects of declined lung function. Around that time, at a doctor's appointment, she got the dreaded words, "you are in chronic rejection." Life as she knew it was over. Her lung function was on rapid decline, and she knew in that moment that her life was changing. Her days of running and hiking were over. She felt an overwhelming sadness and instantly went into mourning over her past life. One day, as she walked through the hospital halls, through tears in her eyes, she saw a man leaning against the wall. His t-shirt said "be strong and courageous," a Bible verse from Joshua 1:9. It just so happens that this has been Jill's verse her entire life. A verse she draws incredible strength from. It was the verse that hung on the wall so she could see it every day during chemo treatments. It was also the verse she wrote on the green ribbon tied to the rope when she rang the bell for her last chemo. That moment, in the hospital hallway, was her reminder that the Lord God is with her wherever she goes. That man leaning against the wall probably just got up that day, put on a shirt and went to a doctor's appointment, but that shirt reminded her that even though she thought her life was over, it wasn't. Jill told me that God is constantly reminding her that she is in covenant with Him, so even if she is not in her comfort zone, she's not alone and that is what gets her through. Later that day, after she saw the t-shirt, she started a new treatment that stopped the decline in lung function. She didn't get any of the lost lung function back, and her life is not as easy as it was pre-rejection, but her life is great! She still has a life expectancy to beat and you can guarantee her faith and fight remain as strong as ever.

Jill's story taught me many things, and caused me to think back about the interactions she and I have shared. When I was a young exercise science college student, she challenged me to pursue my interest in cardiac rehabilitation. She even brought me a book on how to read an electrocardiogram, EKG. In a time when my classmates were trying to decide what they wanted to do with their degree, Jill was guiding me into a specific niche where healthcare and exercise collide. She pushed me to pursue career opportunities, and even let me know when certain jobs were coming available. Even though a medical condition was pushing Jill outside of her comfort zone, she was pushing me outside of mine and others outside of

theirs.

"Let your life experiences mold who you are today."

– Rose Guhr (my amazing wife)

Chapter 6

Daddy!

The Tug

One morning in early 2011 my wife woke up in tears. These tears were not tears of sadness but tears of incredible passion compelling her toward something. She was so emotional that the sound of her sobbing woke me up. "Are you okay?" I asked. Here's me thinking the worst, being pulled out of a deep sleep to the love of my life in tears. My heart racing! She said, "I just had a dream that I was holding a little brown baby boy on the beach...I think we need to go into foster care." Ummm . . . this is not what I expected.

Now, let me back up for a second. You've seen the overall theme of this book right? To continuously challenge your comfort zone because the walls of your zone are flexible. Well, I did not want to test flexibility in this instance; let me explain. Our lives were good. We had a nice home, two kids, good jobs, a great church, great friends and the list goes on. I didn't want any of that to change. MY LIFE WAS COMFORTABLE!!

Figure 2

Here's figure two. Remember, in figure one the character was standing and frustrated. The boundaries set in place were okay because they created a familiar feeling. Still, you'll see the boundaries are the same, with greatness lying equally as far. The character that once stood, is now sitting . . . complacent.

After Rose told me about her dream, she may have asked how I felt about it or what I thought. I'm not sure of my response, but I know I couldn't think straight. She respected that and said we'd give it some time. Weeks went by and we didn't talk about it much, but I couldn't shake what she had told me that morning. God was pulling at me. One evening, Rose and I confessed that we'd both been continually thinking about it and we prayed that God would give us a definitive sign of His intentions during this time of our lives.

The Signs

A couple of days later, I was at work when I got a text from Rose, it was a picture. She had been stopped at a red light and across the intersection was a pickup truck

with the word, in giant letters I might add, FOSTER across

the side of the truck. It was a commercial vehicle for a local

roofing company; interesting, I thought. A few days later,

Rose and I were listening to the radio and a song came on.

We both looked at each other and started smiling, bobbing

our heads and "car dancing." Come on . . . you know what

I'm talking about, we've all done it. It was a catchy tune.

Day after day, we continued to hear this song so we looked

it up to see who the artist was. The name of the band was

Foster the People. Was it coincidence or another sign? To

us, this seemed quite intentional. That next day at work, I

went to the cafeteria to grab some lunch. As I rounded the

corner into the dining area there was a special display of

cupcakes. You know, one of those displays that's not

always there, sort of a limited time only deal. On the side

of the cup cakes were labels that read, Foster and Penn Luxury Cupcakes. There is was again, that word foster. The very next weekend I was on the couch watching a football game. The Houston Texans were playing. I had just tuned in mid-game to see a running play just finishing up. As you might imagine, the camera crew had zoomed in on the player, a common practice in televised games, to highlight the player who had just gained significant yardage. Who was the player? Arian Foster. Foster, right there on the back of his jersey. The instances that you've just read about are common everyday occurrences, but not to us, and not in this particular moment of our lives. God had opened our eyes. We got the message. Rose had been onboard with foster care this entire time. She's the one who had the dream remember? It was me who was not as open. That Sunday, during the football game, I became as open as Rose. It was a difficult admission, but I joined Rose

in opening my hands and we opened our hearts. We

stepped outside of our comfort zones.

Training

If you're not familiar with the process of becoming

a foster parent, let me walk you through it. We decided to

work with a local not-for-profit company named The CALL,

which stands for Children of Arkansas Loved for a Lifetime.

The CALL acts as a liaison between the foster parents and

DHS, the Department of Human Services. Every so often,

The CALL hosts a meeting for those interested in getting

into foster care. Rose and I attended, along with about 25

to 30 others. This meeting was a mixture of information

and experiences. To put it bluntly, it was sort of a step to make sure that we were ready to enter into this journey.

Some people got up and left, others stayed but left

immediately. Afterwards, Rose and I continued looking at

each other throughout the meeting, saying that it doesn't

matter what's said, we were committed, that God had

called us and we knew He would be with us throughout.

After that meeting, we signed up for training. The training

was 40 hours, spread out over the span of several

weekends. Training consisted of a mixture of formal DHS

training along with a special training designed by The CALL.

There was also a period of storytelling on part of those

who were currently fostering kids. We also went through

the background check process and made sure our CPR skills

were up to date. The training consisted of six other families

who were all on track to open their homes at the same

time as we were. Going through this process, you had the

option of being a home for fostering exclusively or you could foster with the option to adopt. We knew God had called us to care for children in our area, but ultimately to bring one of them into our home permanently.

We're Ready

Once we had finished training, we were scheduled for a home visit with a DHS social worker. This was round one. The social worker came to our home, met our children and looked over every square inch of our home. She left us with a list of things to do before her next scheduled visit. This list consisted of many things you would do to ensure the safety of any child of any age who might be in your home. Fortunately for us, our youngest daughter was so young that we had already taken a majority of these safety precautions. What we hadn't done was create a separate space for the child in foster care. This required us to move our daughters into the same bedroom, no big deal; they enjoyed getting to room together. Once our home was ready, the social worker returned for a final walk through. We passed and received a call from DHS a couple days later explaining that we were officially open as a foster home.

Placement

A week went by, no calls. Of course, we were expecting a call from DHS the next day explaining that we had a placement. The call didn't come as soon as expected, so we went about our daily routines of daycare, school, work, dinner and so on. One morning, while I was at work,

I got a phone call from DHS. This was the call we'd been waiting for! It was a social worker from the DHS in nearby Washington County. There was a three-year-old boy who needed placement, and she asked if we had room in our home. Rose and I had discussed this very situation ahead of time so that when the call came, either of us would be ready to accept. I texted Rose immediately, and she responded with a lot of exclamation points. After work, I drove over to the DHS office expecting to meet the newest (even if for a short while) member of our family. He wasn't there yet. Another social worker had just picked him up from his current situation, and they were on their way to the office. When they arrived he was angry. I didn't know what to expect, but put yourself in this little man's shoes for a second. You've just been taken from the only life you knew by a stranger who's doing you a favor, but you don't

89

know that. You're in a strange car, going to a strange place to meet some strange people. I'd be a basket case! This little guy was a mixture of scared out of his mind and angry that he'd been taken from his home. We were introduced as I squatted down to his level. I held out my hand in a high-five motion and he crossed his arms, scowled and said, "I'm not going with you!" Then he stormed off and sat in the corner. Not the introduction I was imagining. I was just exposed to a whole different part of life. There is a harsh world out there and this little dude was caught right in the middle. *It was time for me to be the hands and feet of Jesus*, I thought. Here we go! I went and sat next to him and for the next hour, I did one hundred percent of the talking. He would look at me from time to time as we looked at books, watched a few minutes of The Little Mermaid, and told some jokes. By that time, he and I were cool. We headed toward the car to load up, and the social worker handed me his belongings. A diaper box containing only a pair of socks and a pair of pajamas. We were ready for this because the training had prepped us for the possibility that those coming into our care might not have much. We had a stash of items for a wide range of ages at home. These items had come from The CALL closet, a place where others in the foster care community would contribute items for other foster parents to use.

When we got home, you can imagine he was pretty standoffish, even sticking his tongue out at Rose, but he slowly warmed up. We ate some dinner and called it a night. I got the little guy tucked into his bed, told him goodnight and started to walk out of the room. "Hey!", he yelled before I got to the door. "Sit down by my bed", he ordered. So I sat down speculating that he wanted me to hang with him for a bit longer; I was right. I sat for about five minutes then got up to leave. I made it about half way down the hall when he called again. I went back in and sat down. He closed his eyes but only for about three seconds at a time. After about another five minutes, I stood up but only got that far before, "hey," another call. This time more of a soft inquiry, not a demand. I asked him if he wanted me to stay in there the whole night, he nodded. I grabbed a pillow from the closet and got as comfortable as I could. That was a long night, floors are hard. The next day, we started our typical routine, breakfast, daycare drop off, work, school, daycare pickup and now back home for dinner. This time he was starting to warm up a little bit more to the family. He and the girls played, watched some TV, and Rose read him a couple books. Things were going well. That night I thought I'd rather not sleep on the floor again, so we moved his little bed into our room. We got him tucked in and Rose and I climbed into our bed. When I lay down, guess what I heard? "Hey." I propped myself up with one arm and Rose did the same. "Stay like that," he said. He then proceeded to lay down but open his eyes and check to make sure I didn't move about every five seconds. This continued for about fifteen minutes. After a little while, the time in which he checked on me lengthened until he was sound asleep. The next evening after work and school, we got a visit from the DHS social worker assigned to the little guy's case. She was pleased to see he was in a good environment. That night, we settled in for what was sure to be a slow start to sleep but to our surprise, he laid down, closed his eyes and went right to sleep. Of course, now we were the ones who couldn't go to sleep right away because we kept checking on him. Funny how that works.

He was acclimating to this new environment, and that made us happy. The fourth day would be last time we would see him. Training had taught us that at anytime we could get a call from DHS, stating the child was being placed with a relative. Knowing this, we put a picture of our family in his box of belongings and that box went with him to daycare each day. After dropping him off, we went about our day. That afternoon while I was at work, I got a call from DHS stating that he was being placed with an aunt, and his social worker was in route to get him from daycare. He was our first exposure to the world of foster care. It was hard not getting to say an official goodbye, but we could rest assured that we played an important role in his life, even if it was for three and a half days.

Our Next Placement

That evening, we put things back in order and prepared for the call that would announce our next placement. The next day was fairly uneventful, no call from DHS. The following day, however, was a bit different. On this Saturday in October, Rose and my mom had gone out to check on some local garage sales. It was unseasonably cold and sleeting that morning. Later that day, we got a call from DHS. This time it was an eleven-month-old boy and we were ready for him. He arrived that evening around six. He was asleep in his car seat and was accompanied by a backpack with one diaper and one pair of clothes picked up by the social worker on her way to get him. His carrier was saturated with old crusty formula and smelled of urine. The DHS worker stated that he'd probably be in our care for about a week, that there was a grandmother they were considering for a more permanent placement until his mother could take him back. After she left, we let this little guy sleep as long as he would. Our youngest daughter was about 18 months old, so it hadn't been too long ago that we'd had a baby in the house. As he started to wake up, I knelt down and picked him up from his carrier. He looked at me and said, "Daddy!" Wow! So that's who I was to him in that moment. Welcome to the family, little man, if only for a while. A week went by and DHS called to say that the Grandmother wished for him to stay with his current foster family, us, because she knew he was well cared for. Even though she had no idea who we were, she stated that she could not care for him because she was already caring for his sister, and that would be too much to handle financially. Notifying us of this change in plan, DHS stated that he would be with us for a bit longer. One week turned into two, then three and then four. This little guy was turning one, time to throw a party! A month or so later, he started walking . . . another milestone. Weeks turned into months, and it became apparent that he would be with us for some time. Court date after court date, supervised visit after supervised visit, mid-November came around again, which meant it was time to throw another birthday party and check off yet another milestone. There was a point at which we thought he was going to leave our home. The social worker said we needed to gather his things, that he was going to move in with his birth mother because she had been doing well. The evening before he was to leave, DHS called back. His birth mother had relapsed and he would be staying with us for a while longer. God's plan for his life was playing out, and we could see it in motion everyday. After a lot of emotion and trying times, the state determined that it was in this little man's best interest that he become a ward of the state and eligible for adoption. Two weeks after that court hearing, we became his forever family. We gained a son that day and our girls got a brother.

A Dream made Reality

We adopted our son Zayne in the winter of 2014, a day we've celebrated every year since as his "gotcha day." That next summer in July, we headed to the beach for what would turn into our annual summer vacation tradition. We had been there for about four days when one afternoon, with the sun at its peak, we were all down in the sand building castles and splashing in the ocean. Rose

was admiring how tan Zayne had become and she said,

"he's so dark." In that moment, she remembered her

dream three years earlier; that morning she woke up in

tears having dreamt she was holding a little brown boy on

the beach. This was her dream turned into reality.

TIP: Whether it's you challenging your comfort zone or not,

don't ignore a call on your life. This call will likely challenge

you in ways you can't imagine but also know that when

100

you're faced with hardships, you'll be in the right mindset

to deal with them. Your comfort zone walls are flexible and

sometimes it's not you who is pushing them.

Chapter 7

Rough Water

We have always been an adventurous family. In the Summer of 2018, we decided to take a break from the traditional Florida beach vacation and take our kids to New York City. Rose and I had been to the Big Apple a couple of years before that to attend a cousin's wedding. While we were there, we went to the Macy's Thanksgiving Day parade, enjoyed the Christmas lights at Rockefeller Center, saw the sights, and so on. We enjoyed the city so much that we decided we needed to bring the family back.

Of course we did all the prep we could before we left. We planned each of the eight days we would spend there; where we would stay and eat, how we would travel to and from the hotel and which sites we would see on which days. Even though we were prepared for this kind of a trip; how prepared can you really be taking three kids to the Concrete Jungle? Needless to say, we were ready to roll with the punches. Our first partial day was pretty much the get settled type of day. We found our hotel in Queens, walked around a bit, and even found a great little Mediterranean restaurant. The next morning, we made our first trek into Manhattan with the end goal of taking a ferry boat from the southern tip of the island to the beaches of Sandy Hook, New Jersey. Our boat was scheduled to leave at eleven in the morning so we didn't have much time to waste. After taking in a nice continental breakfast, we packed our backpacks for the day and headed south. Smooth sailing at first and we were following the GPS on our phone. We found the first train from Queens into the city, made our second connection near Times Square and then headed downtown. After exiting the train near the World Trade Center Memorial, the GPS said to head over the Brooklyn Bridge so that's where the five of us went. If you've ever had the chance to walk over the Brooklyn Bridge, you'll know how beautiful it is, but you'll also know how long it is by foot and how crowded. We were about halfway across the bridge, and at a good pace I might add, when I looked down and back in the direction we had just come from. I saw our ferry boat at its dock. I immediately got concerned and had that gut feeling we were heading in the wrong direction. At the pace we were moving, we would have gotten across the bridge and down to the dock in time for departure with some time to spare. However, being mid-bridge, I had a very good visual of our current situation. Every so often along the bridge there were NYPD officers stationed, so we back-tracked as quickly as we could to the nearest officer and he confirmed my

suspicion. We were indeed heading in the wrong direction!

Now we were behind schedule having to go back across

the bridge, against pedestrian traffic flow I might add.

When we reached the base of the bridge, was the dock just

right there? Of course not . . . we had to navigate more city

streets to reach the water's edge and find OUR ferry boat

in a line of about twenty other ferries. We were running at

this point, drenched in sweat, my wife carrying our seven-

year-old daughter, me our six-year-old son and our eleven-

year-old doing her best to keep up. We made it to the

ticket booth, handed in our prepaid voucher and he closed

the booth. The fog horn blared and we were the last

people onto the boat.

We were meeting some family at the beaches, my

wife's cousins and their families. We'd been coordinating

this rendezvous for months and the day was finally here. Some family had to drive several hours to meet us, so missing this boat would not have been good. After finding a seat, we all took a deep breath. Little did we know, our excitement was just beginning.

It was an incredibly windy day; so windy in fact that when we boarded the boat, the captain announced we were under a sea vessel advisory and it could be a rough ride. We started off relatively smooth because of still being in the upper bay which took us past the Statue of Liberty. As we crossed under the Verranzano-Narrows bridge, the bridge that connects the southern tip of Brooklyn with Staten Island, we hit open water and picked up speed. We were sitting in the interior portion of the boat at the front. It rose and sunk with each wave. The further we got into open water, the more intense the boat's movements became. My wife and I joked that we were on an episode of Deadliest Catch. Each time the boat dropped off of a wave, the water would splash up and the wind would slam it along the windows with intense force. There was about a ten-minute period where we could not see outside due to being constantly pummeled by water. After a little while, the intensity of the boat ride seemed to calm down some and my wife and son went outside to the upper deck to look around. They weren't gone long, because the wind picked up again and we went back to the crazy up and down. When she and Zayne were making their way back to their seats, we hit a massive wave, and the boat went side ways. Some people fell out of their seats. Others were screaming, and the trash cans fell over and unfortunately so did Zayne. His head grazed a nearby chair and at that instant he got extremely sea sick. He turned a shade of green that I've not seen in a long time. I'm not sure how he

didn't release everything that was inside of him, but he

didn't. He must have an iron stomach. When we reached

our destination, no one else got off the boat. Apparently,

we were the only ones who cared for a beach trip on this

day. There was another destination down the island, more

of a city atmosphere that everyone else was headed to.

Once off the boat, we all began to feel better and we met

up with our family. The impact of the weather that day was

definitely felt. Producing barren beaches, empty parking

lots, and vacant roads, but we made the most of it. We

walked through a sand-filled path to the beach. Our kids

played in the ocean and we took pictures with the New

York City skyline as our backdrop. We took a guided tour

through the Fort Hancock military compound and got to

walk through a museum/gift shop belonging to the oldest

lighthouse in America. We had a great time. When it came time to head back to mainland New York, we were all a bit leery about the boat ride, but by that time the wind had calmed and we had a nice return ride.

TIP: Challenge your comfort zone on purpose. The walls of your comfort zone are flexible and how do you keep something flexible? By continually moving and stretching. Whenever we do this, we are not guaranteed a smooth experience. Sometimes we will encounter "rough water". Just by taking this trip, we anticipated challenges and at the same time knew we could overcome them. When you approach a challenge with that type of mindset, that there will be some obstacles, you will already have your sights set on a positive outcome.

Chapter 8

Adventure

Take this quick example into mind. If someone throws something at you or to you, what do you do? Well, that depends on what was just thrown right? Is it a beach ball? You catch it or bump it out of the way. Is it a baseball? You put your glove up and snatch it out of the air. Is it a Frisbee? You track it, make a quick snag, and sling it back. Is it a rock? DUCK! Recognizing the obstacle is the first quality to adaptation; being able to react appropriately is the second. You'll find that adaptation is a skill to be strengthened, and a quality to be honed. The key, however, is how often you allow yourself an opportunity to practice. Sometimes, when life throws you a curve ball, you might not know what to do at first, but at least you were at the plate. This brings me into my next story.

I've always enjoyed the outdoors but navigating nature for an extended period of time was not something I'd ever done. On the other hand, Rose's brother Tag was quite the outdoorsman. I look up to him a lot, and always have. I admire his confidence, whether in the woods, on the water, making a fire, setting up a tent, the list goes on. On this particular trip, he and I were going to traverse approximately 35 miles of river via canoe. It was early April and winter was hanging on longer than I would have liked. I'd never done a float and camp combo trip so he had to give me quite a few pointers. Below are the contents of my packing:

- Sleeping bag rated to zero-degrees
- Dry bag to store all contents
- Canned goods (I should have packed double what I did)
- Several changes of clothes
- River shoes
- Poncho

I had to bring a minimalist's mindset to packing. I'm sharing a canoe, not an SUV. Plus, we had a tent and a few other miscellaneous items with us.

The morning of the take off came so I drove in the dark to his house. We loaded up and headed to our entry point, about an hour upriver. Also going along with us on this trip were two friends. Once the four of us made it to our starting point, we unpacked our gear and unloaded the canoes. Before we could start, however, we had to position our shuttle situation. Tag and a friend drove two vehicles to our takeout point, left a vehicle there and drove back together so we would have a vehicle at each end of our trip. Positioning the shuttle vehicles took about two hours because of where they had to drive. Remember, we were floating a long way, in Arkansas. The roads aren't exactly a straight shot. We finally got on the river mid-morning. It was an overcast day and maybe forty degrees. I was fully dressed in a sweatshirt, jeans, socks and shoes, a stocking hat and gloves. I was cold! I sat in the front of the canoe, all of our gear in the middle and Tag was in the back. If you've not ridden in a canoe before, the more experienced of the two in the canoe sits in the back to guide and steer the boat. We had been floating for a few hours when we came to a point in the river where there were some cliffs and rock formations. We decided to stop and take a break because it had been raining on us for a while and even though I had a poncho on, being wet and cold is not a fun combination. I could hardly feel my toes and fingers from sitting idle in the canoe. We hiked up to a little covering in the rocks where we found some dry sticks and brush and made a fire. It was the best fire I've ever felt! I got to thaw out my hands a bit, and it was good for my soul. We also found a really nice machete someone had left behind; this would come in handy later on. We continued floating until late evening, about 12 miles, and stopped to make camp for the night. By this time, my toes were pretty much numb again, and I was starving. No surprise really, I eat a lot on a normal day, but on this day I had burned quite a few calories. It wasn't from a lot of activity (yes I did some paddling), but mostly from freezing my butt off! First, we made a fire to warm us up, and then we put up the tent. Dinner that night was canned ravioli. I put the can straight onto the coals and whittled a sort of spoon/fork out of a stick. Okay, it was really more of a pointed stick and I skewered the ravioli, so it worked fine. That night was an interesting one. The temperature dropped to below freezing. It was cold in the tent, even in a zero degree sleeping bag, but we experienced the temperature outside of our tent when we awoke to yelling. "The boats, the boats! They're going to float away!" Our friends had woken up to their tent laying in about two inches of water. Due to the fact it rained a majority of our float that first day, the river was on the rise. Tag and I had set up our tent a little higher so we were okay, but the river had now reached our friend's tent, and our canoes were less than five minutes from being swept down the river. We got the canoes pulled up to higher ground, and they moved their tent. We tried to salvage what sleep we could get before dawn. The next morning, the river was a sight to be seen. It had risen about two feet overnight and was moving fast! We hurried to take down our tent, load the canoes and eat a granola bar. I was a bit nervous getting on the water that morning, as I'd never floated on that swift of a current, but we didn't really have a choice.

Day two on the river was great. The sun came out and it didn't rain. This was to be our longest day on the river. We planned to go about 15 miles, and with the high water level, we knew we'd make good time. We navigated some pretty gnarly rapids that day. I can still close my eyes and picture one rapid sequence in particular where we had to make quite a few turns due to trees blocking the traditional river route. Tag shouted commands behind me: "Paddle left. Now right! Hold on . . . paddle right, drag left!" It was intense. Tag's end of the canoe didn't have a built-in seat, so he brought along a folding chair. As we traversed the rapids, he was in a hover position, slightly above his chair giving him more agility and maneuvering capability. We made a sharp turn just around some parts of a tree that had recently fallen after an ice storm the previous winter. The branches caught his chair and pulled it over board. I think he ended up sitting on the edge of the canoe the remainder of the trip. There were even several times we had to cut our way through trees that had fallen and completely blocked the river. I remember hacking a path through brush so we could keep going. Thank you to the machete we had found the day before. At one juncture in the river, we came to a low water bridge. Typically, we would have floated under it, but not that day. The water was so high that we only saw the bridge because of the dirt road on either side. Also, Tag knew it was there because he'd floated that section of river before. What we couldn't see, however, was about a three-foot drop on the other side of the bridge. Because of the weight of our boat and the gear we had in it, we decided not to chance it, so we walked around. Night two was much more calm. It was a clear night. The stars were out, the temperature was mild and the river didn't rise. A mild breeze and the sound of the river combined for a good night's sleep.

On the third day, the river was still moving at a good pace and the sun was shining bright. Because of the mileage we'd put in the previous two days, the third day would be much shorter, only about six miles. An uneventful, peaceful float. After setting up camp that evening we did some swimming and played catch with a frisbee. The next day, day four, we finished our float. This day reminded me of the first, cool temperatures, overcast skies, and windy. Tag left with the others to get the other vehicle, I pulled the boats up and made a fire to keep myself occupied until their return. About two hours later he showed back up with a full plate of fried catfish, hushpuppies and a large soda. WOW! That was a fantastic meal. Being on the river takes a toll. I was drained and completely out of food by the time we finished, having used every bit of energy to help push us to our destination. The meal Tag brought back for me vanished in a hurry.

I was thankful for a good trip. It was nice to take a break from the hustle and bustle of life and soak up time with nature. That trip was definitely outside of my comfort zone. What did I learn? That new experiences bring about new skills. Adaptation was my key takeaway, and that skill has served me well in both my personal and professional life.

TIP: When a challenge comes your way, you learn how to navigate around it. When an obstacle comes at you in your life, think about the tree in the rapids. Do you let it take you out, along with the chair? Of course not; you crouch down, adjust your stance, and keep moving forward. What about the unseen bridge? Some of life's biggest challenges come upon us without warning. Sometimes we get little hints that they exist and sometimes these are the trickiest to traverse. Rely on your ability to sense the need for change and adapt accordingly. Sometimes you might have to take your boat completely around an obstacle in order to proceed forward. Remember that the walls of your zone are flexible. Reach out with your paddle (or your machete!) and create some new space around yourself.

Figure 3

Do you ever feel like the character in the figure
above? Happy and comfortable with how things are, yet,
peering out to see what type of greatness lies ahead? If
that's you, you are not alone. Many people feel this.
There's nothing wrong with feeling this way. As you
progress through this book, take not of how the figure and
character change.

"If you get into the habit of just being mediocre, it will become part of your consciousness."

-Believe You Can Do It, a motivational video on YouTube

A Trip to India

Remember Clayton? The small-town Oklahoman who was shoved involuntarily from his comfort zone by his Deputy Chief of Police, Bill? Well, later on in his career he stepped out of his comfort zone voluntarily. No one pushed him, imagine that? The young detective who was afraid to give a few speeches was about to take on a much bigger commitment. That's the funny thing about comfort zones; as they grow, so do you. Clayton, now a seasoned law enforcement agent, found himself once again called into his superior's office. This time the president of the Rotary Club was present as well. The Rotary Club president proceeded to tell Clayton about a rare, all-expenses-paid opportunity to travel abroad. This trip was designed for someone to travel alone for six weeks, staying with different families for several days at a time. The participant would keep notes of experiences along the way and report back upon returning. He was not given any information about his destination or the families that would host him. He was only told that the Rotary had already scheduled the stops he would make, and that he would be safe and taken care of. If interested, he would be one of four applicants to be interviewed by a panel of community leaders. Of the four, three of them would receive further preparation. Ultimately one would be chosen for the trip. The day of the interview came, and Clayton was the first one out. A member of the panel told him that because he was in law enforcement, he was not flexible enough to take the trip; a bias not too well received by Clayton. Clayton deliberated for a long moment before answering. "Yes, I might seem rigid," he said. "But that's because when I pull someone over for a traffic violation and decide to give a ticket, I'm not changing my mind, you're getting a ticket. If I decide I'm taking someone to jail, they're going to jail and I'm not changing my mind. But let me tell you about flexibility. Each morning when I wake up, I have no idea what my day will look like. I have to be ready for whatever comes at me. That mindset puts me in a position to be able to handle what comes my way." The panel member consulted with the others and decided that Clayton could be an alternate. So at this point, they basically still had three individuals ahead of him. The chances of him taking the trip were slim to none. Clayton attended each training session, completed each assignment, and learned as much as he could. During the training, one member dropped out, and another had an unforeseen circumstance arise. That left just one other person and Clayton. Well, unfortunately, near the end of the training, the other person got sick, and that left only Clayton. You see, he had placed himself in a position of readiness. He could have accepted "fourth place" way back at the interview. How many people would have simply gone on with their life? Would you have? Clayton's comfort zone had expanded so much that the word defeat didn't mean near as much as it once might have. Even if it didn't seem likely that he'd make the trip, he still wanted to learn, and as fate would have it, that "go go go" mentality we spoke to in chapter four put him in prime position for a once-in-a-lifetime experience. He ended up traveling to India. He lived in huts with dirt floors and houses without running water. He experienced all modes of travel and worked alongside the host families who accepted him as their own. While he was immersing himself into the Indian culture, his comfort zone was expanding even further.

Expansion Strategies

Too often we try to accomplish a monster feat, and if we fall short of the goal we feel we've failed. We may even stop trying. So to help you in your quest for glory, try the following things I call the COMFORT ZONE EXPANSION STRATEGIES (did you hear that in a loud boisterous announcer's voice with an echo? I did). Read it again, COMFORT ZONE EXPANSION STRATEGIES, **STRATEGIES, STRATEGIES.**

- Do you want to improve your health? Start small, and go for a five-minute walk one evening a week. Or set an alarm to do five push-ups each morning after waking up. On Sundays, prep fruits and veggies into easy-grab baggies for your week ahead. In James Clear's book Atomic Habits, he explains the "how to" when starting a new habit. Atomic Habits speaks to the fact that you have to first become the type of person who walks every evening, does push-ups everyday or eats fruits and veggies with every meal. Start small, become the type of person who creates habits.

- Tired of hitting the snooze button? Put your alarm across the room so you're forced to get out of bed to turn it off. I had a bad habit of doing that, so I put my phone across the room, forcing me to physically move in order to turn the alarm off.

- Interested in leadership? Find a "quick read" book focusing on leadership characteristics. Do you have a commute into work each day? Most do. Utilize technology to listen to a podcast or an audio book. Take advantage of this time to absorb and learn, adding value to a time otherwise wasted. Walk into work engaged, not aggravated. If you want to lead others, you must first lead yourself.

- Have you thought of rekindling an old friendship? Invite them out for coffee or lunch. Maybe even to your home for dinner. What if they don't live close by? Simply send a text message or reach out on social media.

- Are you passionate about growing in a certain profession? Reach out to the person who's currently in the position you aspire to be in. I've done this on numerous occasions and found that those individuals have been more than happy to spend time sharing their hard-earned knowledge.

- What if you're looking for adventure? Go on a zip lining tour or schedule that trip you've always wanted to take. Look up some local hiking trails or go horseback riding. Anything to push your limits a little. It's a big world!

- Are you looking to be more involved in your community? Volunteer at your local food bank, or call a local school district and get scheduled to be a guest reader.

The list can go on, but what I'm getting at is the common thread between all of these things: intentionality! If you are going to expand your comfort zone, you have to do it on purpose.

"You can make excuses or you can make progress but you can't make both." – Craig Groeschel

Chapter 9

Beyond Boundaries

Boundaries are good. They keep us safe. Physical boundaries can be as simple as a line painted on the road to help drivers stay on the correct side. Or boundaries can be as sharply drawn as the wall that separates a powerful tiger from a fascinated toddler. The bases clear when the baseball sails over a particular wall. Fences make a good neighbor. Emotional boundaries are also good. They protect our feelings. They create a healthy space between a boss and an employee, and they guard our hearts from being hurt. While boundaries are often seen as a safeguard, they also can provide a roadmap for growth. What are some boundaries in your life? Identifying your boundaries is a key step in comfort zone expansion. While we need some boundaries to remain in place, some are simply roadblocks you've allowed to get in the way of unleashing greatness in your life. Once you figure out which boundaries need to stay and which ones can be moved, you'll be on your way!

In early 2014, I identified a boundary that needed to move. I had put up a wall around our family. As the husband and father, that's what I'm supposed to do right? I'm the protector. We had a nice home, good jobs, two reliable vehicles, and three amazing kids (you read about them already). We had a good church and great friends. Our parents and siblings were close. It was a safe atmosphere. Why on earth would I mess that up? That boundary wasn't built overnight. It was constructed piece by piece. Day after day, solidifying the fact that we were in a good place. In the introduction of this book, I posed a question, "how long is good, good enough?" I can tell you the defining moment that changed my thought process that spring, but if I really think about it, my wife's heart along with mine had been preparing long before that moment. I got a call from a former boss, Jill, you read about her in chapter four. When I was getting my undergraduate degree, she and I worked together. She was the manager of a local fitness center and I, a young fitness specialist. Jill and I connected through a common professional interest. I was interested in caring for individuals suffering from heart disease and it just so happened that Jill had her Master's degree in Exercise Physiology, specializing in the same focus. We spent hours at work talking about the field of cardiac rehabilitation. After I graduated and my family and I moved so I could attend my internship in cardiac rehab, Jill moved as well. She moved to Tulsa, Oklahoma to take an exercise physiologist position in cardiac rehab. When Jill called in the Spring of 2014, she set in motion a change that our hearts were ready for. She had heard of a hospital looking for a Cardiac Rehab Department Manager. She thought I would be a good fit, and she encouraged me to apply. As my wife and I discussed the possibility, we thought about the big changes ahead. We would have to move. We'd be leaving our friends and our church. We'd be moving further from family and we would have to sell our house. What would my boss think? What would my co-workers think? So many thoughts ran through our heads, but with each thought came thoughts of change, excitement about the future, possibility. I decided to take the leap and apply for the job. I was mid-way through the application when Jill called. They hired someone else. I was heartbroken, as all of the "what if's" of possibility vanished in a second. The boundaries of safety and protection I had built that were slowly starting to come down, went right back up and were firmer than before. *Nope,* I told myself. *I put myself out there and it didn't work out.* How many times have you said that to yourself? How many times did you stretch or try to expand your comfort zone only to have it "not work out." A few weeks went by, the dust settled, things were back to normal. One afternoon while I was watching Zita at a little gymnastics place in town I got a phone call, it was Jill. Another job opportunity had presented itself in Tulsa. This time it was for a startup weight loss program, and the hospital was looking for a Health Educator. I was intrigued, I didn't know anything about the position, but the thoughts of new opportunities came rushing back in and those boundaries started to lower. Funny how that works, isn't it? The walls of my comfort zone are flexible, just like yours. The more you press, the more flexible they become.

Seems like a common theme. We didn't need to deliberate as long as before. I'm pretty sure I applied the next day. That next week we went on our usual family beach vacation, and while we were in Florida, the department supervisor called requesting an interview. I remember calling my boss at the time and telling her about my interview. I was shaking so bad, not sure how she would react. She was calm and supportive, a lesson I'd hold with me in the years to come. Through a series of in-person and phone interviews, drives to Tulsa and presentations prepared and given, I accepted an offer. We were moving to Tulsa! At this point, the boundary I had previously constructed over the years had now been stripped down to nothing. We were vulnerable, a key character trait you'll find for expanding your zone. The next few weeks were a whirlwind. In a matter of three days, we put our house on the market and saw it go under contract. We immediately started to pack, while I started my new job. My first day as the Health Educator for the Tulsa hospital consisted of boarding a plane for California. I was off to Redondo Beach for training while Rose looked after three kids below the age of eight. She packed up for the move while finishing out the semester at her teaching job. I remember texting back and forth with Rose and a Tulsa realtor between connecting flights. Looking at pictures of houses, putting in offers and signing papers via electronic document. What was happening? We were submitting offers on houses that we hadn't even walked through? This stretch in our lives took a toll on us, but we got through it. When I landed back in Tulsa, I drove to meet the realtor and look at a house before making the two-hour drive home. The house was spacious, twice as big as our current house, and built in the early 80's. It had two stories under a barn style roof. It had been recently remodeled, and had a huge maple tree in the back yard. I thought it was great, I texted some pictures to Rose and then put in an offer. Our offer was accepted before Rose had ever stepped foot in the house. I'll say she definitely put a lot of trust in me. We now had to close on our house in Arkansas and close on the new house in Tulsa. I was staying with a friend in Tulsa during the week and driving to Arkansas on the weekends. Weekends slammed with trying to soak in family time while making sure the house was ready for the sale. When we closed on the Arkansas house, it would still be two weeks until we could close on the house in Tulsa. Where would we stay? Where would we put our "packed to the gills" 26-foot U-haul truck of things? The owners of our soon-to-be-new home were gracious enough to allow us to store our belongings in the garage until closing, and the friends I had been staying with put us up in a townhouse they owned that was vacant at the time. God's faithfulness to us was on display in that season in our lives. We were always taken care of and we definitely grew closer as a family.

Since the move from Arkansas to Oklahoma; I have changed jobs, gotten a Master's degree, and oh, we moved again. The difference this time is that our boundaries look much different. A stiff wall of comfort has been replaced with a flexible sphere of opportunity.

Crazy Socks

One year for my birthday, a co-worker gifted me a pair of argyle socks. They were black with silver diamonds and red trim. My socks before then were plain black dress socks, nothing flashy. Safe. Comfortable. I wore the argyle socks once in a while, and every time I did I got a compliment on them. It made me feel good, so I bought a second pair, then a third pair, a fourth and so on. Now my sock drawer holds mostly crazy and loud socks. My wife even bought me a pair for Valentines Day that have her face and hearts on them! People at work now grade me on the "crazy level" of my socks. One of our volunteers even gave me an article called "The Joy of Socks," written by Connie Cronley. It describes socks as one of life's great unappreciated pleasures. The idea of a sock began when the Egyptians, Romans and Greeks would wrap their feet in fabric or leather. When the knitting machine made its debut in the 16th century, socks became more mainstream. They were made of cotton, and it wasn't until the late 1930s that socks were made from nylon. I clearly know too much about socks, but the point is this: do you go through life playing it safe or do you step out and wear something wild? I'll let you make that call.

Chapter 10

A Road Trip and A Lasting Legacy

I was fourteen years old, it was the summer of 1996 and I was in a lull between basketball camp and the start of the new school year. Now that you have that general idea, I'd like to provide some context before continuing the story.

My Grandpa on my dad's side was a farmer by profession. He had cattle and pigs, along with hundreds of acres that he farmed for crops. He and my Grandma lived on land out in the country. Well, when I was probably ten years old or so he sold all of the land, all of the farm equipment and house. He and my Grandma bought a little house that sat on a small river skirting the outer city limits, and it wasn't long before he took up another profession.

He bought a brand new Ford F250 and began pulling RV's,

campers, all across the country. He would grab an RV from

the dealership in McPherson, Kansas and pull it to the next

destination, wherever that might be. He would then hook

on to another and pull it to a different place, and then pull

an RV back to Kansas. My Grandpa was also part of the

Gideon's ministry. For those unfamiliar with that

organization, they're the group responsible for handing out

those little green bibles. My Grandpa was heavily involved

with his church family. He sang in a men's quartet for many

years and volunteered with the church for as long as I can

remember. When he began pulling RV's, he used that as a

platform for furthering the mission of Jesus, which is to

spread the Gospel to all people. He would pick up

hitchhikers, whenever and wherever he could. When he

picked them up, he would talk with them for a while, learning who they were, where they were going, how it was that they ended up at this particular juncture in life, and so on. Eventually, he would explain who he was. He would hand them a little green bible and tell them about the God he loved and who loved him unconditionally in return. Sometimes the message was received well, sometimes not. Regardless, he carried out his mission to connect with all the people he encountered. He wanted to give them more than a ride; he hoped to change the direction of their lives. When I was fourteen, I got to witness this mission being carried out firsthand.

One sunny morning during that Summer of '96, my Grandpa called the house and explained to my parents that he had an upcoming trip planned to pull an RV to California. He asked if I would like to come along for the

3,300-mile road trip. As I write this book, I am 38 years old. I look back on this one particular instance in my life and realize how this pivotal time helped shape me into the person I am today. It also played a key role in helping me identify the purpose in my career. Legacy has a lot to do with it.

I packed my bags and away we went. The first thing we did was stop at the local Wal-Mart. We bought some snacks for the road and Grandpa also thought I needed some entertainment, so he bought me a Gameboy and two games, Super Mario Bros. and Zelda. Our trip took us through five states, including Kansas and California. I remember driving through the Rocky Mountains of Colorado, stopping at a concrete tree in the salt flats of Utah and cresting over the top of a mountain to see the lights of Las Vegas at night. When we'd find a place to stop for the night, we'd climb into the RV we were pulling to sleep. The particular RV we were pulling to California was a brand new 34-foot, triple axle Alfa Gold. Basically a 5-star hotel on wheels. I'd never seen anything like it. It had three slide outs, two ceiling fans and other high end finishes I'd never seen in a camper.

During the trip I recall picking up at least four hitchhikers. On two separate occasions I sat in the back of the extended cab truck while the hitchhiker sat in the passenger seat. These two occasions were lengthy because I remember sitting back there for a while. On a different occasion, however, I remember stopping to pick up two guys at once. I got to share the extended cab part of the truck that time with someone else. Point being, my Grandpa would pick up however many people he could fit in the truck. Now, I need to include here that on this trip he was probably a little more cautious; since he had his grandson with him. If he didn't feel right about it, we kept going. The guys we picked up threw what belongings they had in the bed of the truck and off we went to their next stop. As I type and recall these particular moments, I think about how different life was – and not that long ago. Today, picking up a hitchhiker is not a common practice. However, on this trip I didn't feel threatened or nervous at all. Okay, small lie, the first guy we picked up, I was a little apprehensive, but I was ready. You see, when we started the trip, Grandpa made me aware of his practice of picking up those on the side of the road asking for a ride. He asked my permission and I agreed. I'm sure there was hesitancy on the part of many people in 1996 when it came to picking up strangers and offering them a ride but where many people might have seen someone walking along the road and kept driving, my Grandpa saw an opportunity to share his love of Jesus.

When we made it to Chico, California, we planned was to unload that RV and begin the trip home to Kansas. I was looking forward to the return trip because it meant that I would get to spend some time with my dad before he went back to work. My mom and sister had planned a girls' trip out of town, so the plan was for my dad and I to go to the movies and hang out when my Grandpa and I returned from California. Well, my Grandpa and I were about halfway home when he got a call from his company that he needed to go get an RV in Chicago, Ill. I remember being bummed, because this meant that we would spend an additional few days on the road and I would miss the opportunity to hang out with my dad. Realizing my disappointment, my Grandpa called the company and informed them that he would not be able to go get that RV because he had to get his grandson home. I'm embarrassed to recount this portion of our trip because of my selfishness. My Grandpa no doubt missed out on a good chuck of money by turning down the trip to Chicago, but I'm also reminded of his selflessness and his love for me.

That trip taught me a lot about life. Did I know that at the time? Of course not. I was just along for the ride, but as I look back now, that trip was grooming me for lessons I would apply later in my life.

My grandfather's comfort zone was massive! Think about it. He was a farmer for 40-plus years. He sold everything, moved to the city and completely changed professions. He picked up strangers along the highway and talked candidly with them as he drove. How could he do this? Maybe because he lived for something beyond himself. His mission on this earth was to fully invest in the lives of others. How many lives did he affect? How many life trajectories did he alter for the better because of a few moments spent in intentional connection? There's one life I know he changed for the better, and that's mine. Today when I think about my life's purpose, it's related directly to intentional investment in relationships. To leave a lasting legacy of purpose on those I interact with. I also want to show my children what the love of Jesus looks like, because I got a first hand demonstration of that with the life led by my Grandfather, Milton Guhr. There's no doubt the flexible walls of my comfort zone moved on that trip, and I'm forever grateful.

Above, you'll see the concrete tree we stopped at in the

Utah salt flats. Also sometimes called the Tree of Life, it

stands 87 feet tall and is located along Interstate 80.

The character in figure four has now decided to make a

change. The character has decided to start challenging the

wall of their comfort zone. You'll notice that where former

boundaries and greatness were once apart, have now

started to merge. The walls are growing and expanding.

"You don't need to climb Mount Everest to feel like

you've accomplished something great."

-Jason Jedamski

Chapter 11

Bringing it Full Circle

If I could harness the best smell in the world, it would be that of a freshly brewed cup of coffee. Oh my goodness! I can see the steam rising up from the cup, encircling my nose and giving it a big kiss, just like the animated odor in the cartoons. Now, to then drink that cup of coffee? Don't mind if I do.

I sat in the lobby of my insurance agent one morning. As I was waiting for our appointment to begin, the receptionist asked if I'd like a cup of coffee while I waited. "Sure, thank you," I said. It just came out of my mouth. *Wait, did I just accept a cup of coffee? I've never done that before,* I thought. Throughout that appointment

I sipped on the coffee until the mug was empty and I thoroughly enjoyed it. That was the first of many cups of coffee I would enjoy. My wife was already a coffee drinker, so now I could join her. We started with just using k-cups, but now we have a coffee pot and grind our own coffee beans. It seems simple and maybe somewhat comical, that I remember the day I learned to love coffee but I'm getting better at living in the moment and reflecting on those moments that are shaping my identity. A lot has changed for me over the years. I don't drink Dr. Pepper anymore, or soda for that matter. I embrace adventure, routinely seek advice from those in positions of leadership and I welcome change. All of these life experiences have created the "me" I am today. Who am I? I am a faith-filled husband to one and a father to three. I love Jesus, my family, my career, coffee, loud socks and intentionally investing in others.

That's who I am, and one thing is for certain, the walls of my comfort zone are very pliable, and I hope yours are heading in that direction as well. What defines you? If you think about it for a second, you might surprise yourself. My guess is, you've come a lot farther than you know, and best part? You are one stretch away from achieving something great!

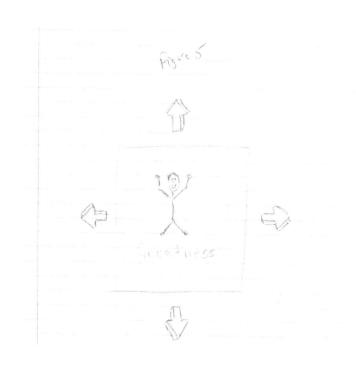

The character in figure five is you. You've stretched and challenged the walls of your comfort zone. You're excited about what you've done and feel a great sense of fulfillment. You'll notice that the walls of your newly formed zone are not fixated on recent achievement, but still pliable and ready to swallow up more!

159

Acknowledgments

I want to thank my wife, Rose, for inspiring me to be better each day. Thank you for keeping me focused on this project, and in life, and asking me from time to time, "When was the last time you worked on your book?" It's finished! You are my rock, my best friend, and I look forward to many more adventures with you. Thank you to Zita, Zoe and Zayne, our three amazing kids, for bringing joy into our lives; Mama and Daddy love you! Thank you to my parents for raising me in a Christian home and for teaching me a strong work ethic. Thank you to Clayton, Natalie and Jill for sharing your stories with the readers of this book. The message in your words brought great value to my life. I want to thank my grandparents for the lives they led and the legacy they left through the lives of my parents. Thank you to Tag Ellis for being a fantastic brother-in-law and to Rose's dad for always being there for us and for being a super cool GrandDude to your grandkids. A final thank you to those cited in this book. Your devotion to leadership and your investment into others either through book, podcast, interview or work has afforded me great opportunities to learn and grow.

References

www.usmarshals.gov. History – Broad Range of

History

2020, The Last Dance, Michael Jordan Documentary

produced by ESPN Films and Netflix

Clear, James. 2018. Atomic Habits; Tiny Changes,

Remarkable Results; An Easy & Proven Way

to Build Good Habits & Break Bad Ones.

Alexander, Scott. 1980. Rhinoceros Success.

Heath, Chip and Dan. The Power of Moments; Why

Certain Experiences Have Extraordinary

Impact

www.treeofutah.com

www.elbingks.com

The YouVersion Bible App

www.twistedsifter.com; Teacher Fills Hallway with

Balloons to Give Students a Lesson on

Happiness.

Cronley, Connie. 2018. TulsaPeople.com; The Joy of

Socks; One of the great unappreciated

pleasures of life is socks.

www.fearlessmotivation.com